OSWESTRY
PARISH CHURCH
its early history

by
John Pryce-Jones

Llanforda Press
1992

ACKNOWLEDGEMENTS

The author is grateful for the assistance provided by the National Trust and the Courtauld Institute of Art (for permission to reproduce the portrait of Sir Thomas Myddelton); the National Library of Wales (for permission to reproduce the portrait of Bishop Morgan); Chichester Public Library (for providing the illustration of Thomas FitzAlan's tomb, from Tierney's *History of Arundel*); the members of staff of the Shropshire Local Studies Library, Shrewsbury; Ruby Bacha and Pat Ireson.

Front cover: Hugh Yale, as represented by the Yale Monument, situated in the north aisle of Oswestry parish church. Alderman Yale's burial, within the church, is recorded in the parish register for January 9th, 1606.

BRITISH LIBRARY CATALOGUING-IN-PUBLICATION DATA
A catalogue record for this book is available from the British Library.

ISBN 0 9517162 1 2

Printed by Sayce Brothers, Llandrindod Wells

FOREWORD

by the Rev. D. B. Crowhurst, Vicar of Oswestry Parish Church

I am glad to commend this short history of Oswestry's historic parish church, where Christians have worshipped for nearly 1,000 years.

At the time of writing , Project 2000–an ambitious plan of Restoration–has been in operation for three years, having been launched at Eastertide 1989. Phase I, the restoration of the Tower, is complete (and nearly paid for) and the parish is turning its attentions to the electrics, with a general rewiring and relighting scheme.

In the future, attention will have to be given to the Roof, the Mullions and Windows, and Drainage. With an ancient building, there is always work to be seen to.

But the Eucharist exhorts, "Send us out into the world, to live and work to Thy praise and glory." St Oswald's is a power-house where the Gospel is preached, so that God's love may be shown to his people. Worshippers, visitors and pilgrims pass through its doors in the tradition of the footsteps of the last 1,000 years, and, we hope and pray, will continue to do so well into the next 1,000.

February 1992

AUTHOR'S INTRODUCTION

This booklet can be traced back to the written notes which were the basis of a talk given by the author to members of the Oswestry & Border History & Archaeology Group in April 1991. Those notes have been revised and, in part, completely rewritten. Additional sections have been inserted, and a number of illustrations, both old and new, have been added to complement the written word.

The subject of the original lecture was the history of Oswestry parish church from earliest times through to the close of the 17th century. This booklet covers the same period; readers should note that it does not, therefore, consider the great restoration work carried out by the Victorians, or the life and work of St. Oswald's during the present century. Readers seeking information upon these more recent periods in the church's history should refer to present-day guidebooks of the church, and to John Askew Roberts' eye-witness description of the architect G. E. Street's transformation of St Oswald's, printed in the *Transactions of the Shropshire Archaeological Society* for 1880.

Oswestry parish church–its early history is published 1,350 years after the martyrdom of King Oswald; just over 900 years after the parish church's foundation; and 300 years after the completion of the repair and rebuilding necessitated by the Civil War. The booklet can be said to cover 1,000 years of the ecclesiastical history of Oswestry in the space of 32 pages. It cannot, therefore, claim to be comprehensive; its purpose is to review each of the main themes in the church's early history, including its foundation, its links with Shrewsbury Abbey, the impact upon St Oswald's of the dissolution of the monasteries and of the English Reformation, and the effect upon the church fabric of the Civil War. Readers wishing to delve further should follow up the notes and references to source material, listed on pages 28-31.

The Llanforda Press has published this booklet in association with Oswestry parish church's Project 2000 appeal, so as to raise funds for St Oswald's refurbishment and restoration.

OSWESTRY PARISH CHURCH–ITS EARLY HISTORY

It may be appropriate to begin with the observations of two illustrious visitors to Oswestry. Nikolaus Pevsner would have visited the town in the mid-1950s whilst researching his *Buildings of England* volume upon Shropshire. [1] He described St Oswald's as "A large church facing Church Street with three parallel gables, but a church in which the Victorian contribution dominates. The big and strong tower at the south west end is in its lower part of the 13th century, in its upper parts with balustrade and eight pinnacles of the late 17th century after the church had suffered badly in the Civil War." Pevsner then directs his readers' attention briefly to a simple 13th century window next to the tower, at the west end, and to the east chancel and the north aisle windows, "supposed to be correct reproductions." He adds the comment, "All the rest is by G. E. Street, 1872-4, and not one of Street's masterpieces", and that, in the main, is Oswestry's ancient parish church dealt with.

Pevsner's tour of inspection was preceded, over 400 years earlier, by that of John Leland–traveller, court librarian, priest, and the 'father' of English topography–who visited Oswestry in the late 1530s. Leland noted that "the Chirch of St Oswalde is a very faire leddid church with a great tourrid steple, but it standith without the New-Gate; so that no chirch is there withyn the towne. This chirche was sumtime a monasterie caullid the White Minster. After turnid to a paroche chirch, and the personage inpropriate to the abbey of Shreusbyri. The cloister stoode in the memory of men where there are monuments to monks. The place and streate wer the chirch standithe is caullid Stretllan." He continued, "There be chapelles clene without the suburbes. One betwixt Stratllan and Porth de (chapel of St John the Baptist). The secund without the same suburbe within a bow shot of S. Oswalde (St Oswald's chapel, where Oswald's Well is situated). The third north est toward Chester (of St Edith)." Writing of St Oswald's Well, Leland added that "Ther is a chapel over it of tymber and the fountein environed with a stone wall." Leland's description includes various details relating to the legend of St Oswald, and, in the margin, he added the note, "Fair walkes about St Oswaldes Welle." Finally, Leland noted that the Morda river "riseth in a hille caullid Llanvarda wher was a chirch now decaid. Sum say this was the paroch chirch of Oswestre." [2]

In a concise manner, and an authoritative style, Leland's commentary touches upon most of the themes running through St Oswald's early history: the church's origins, its supposed monastic connections, its chapels, its shape and its appearance. However, an authoritative style and manner should not deceive. Leland took pains to be cautious with his description, utilising words and phrases such as "sum say ", "sumtime" and "within living memory." Leland is a very valuable source–for a pre-Civil War description of Oswestry parish church he is the only real source–but he has to be used with caution.

For instance, Leland's reference to "cloisters" and "monuments to monks" has encouraged successive generations of historians and commentators upon the parish church to link King Oswald's martyrdom in 642 A.D. to the foundation of a monastery close to the battlefield. Thus Thomas Pennant, in 1784, described how "a church arose on the place of martyrdom, dedicated to the saint. A monastery was founded, which bore the name of Blanc-minster, Candida ecclesia, Album monasterium, and White-minster." He continued, "It is very singular that no evidences exist, either of the time of the foundation or of the dissolution. The last must have happened in Saxon days, for, immediately after the Conquest, the church of St. Oswald was bestowed on the abbey of Shrewsbury. Bishop Tanner doubts whether there ever was a monastery here: but the authority of Leland puts this much out of the question."[3]

St Oswald's south western tower. The uppermost storey, above the clock face, post-dates the Civil War; the lower storeys are mediaeval, though much restored over the centuries.

Leland also suggested that there had been, in former times, a church at Llanforda, and that this church had been the district's first parish church. Although this suggestion appears somewhat unlikely, it must be acknowledged as a theory current in Oswestry during the 1530s. The theory survived into the 17th century, being cited by the Recorder, John Davies of Middleton, in his *Observations on the antient and moderne names of the Towne and Borrough of Oswestrie*, completed in 1635. Davies wrote that, "I have a note taken out of some anonimous author", telling how Reyner, the early 13th century Bishop of St Asaph, had "suppressed the ould church of the Mercians called by the Brittaines Llanvorda (that is the temple or church of the Ordovices) which was distant about a mile of

Oswestry." It has been claimed[4] that Mr Davies was suggesting that the element 'Forda' or 'Morda' in the place-name Llanforda was derived from 'Mercia'; in fact, he was arguing that the name Llanforda referred to the British tribe, the Ordovices. Another explanation of the name Llanforda is that the 5th century Welsh chieftain Mordaf Hael was the founder of this mysterious church;[5] in this theory's favour, it might be noted that the place-name often appears in early written records spelt 'Llanfordaf'. Certainly the name suggests the presence of a church, but no evidence at all has been found beyond the place-name itself. In any case, the likelihood that any such church, chapel or cell, located in the upper Morda valley, or on the slopes above, moved down to Oswestry is difficult to credit. Furthermore, one might suspect that, had there been any real validity to the story, then the curiosity of Edward Lloyd, the last of the Lloyds of Llanforda, or of his antiquarian son Edward Lhuyd, would have been aroused. One suspects that the element 'llan' in the name, quite possibly corrupted from something else, has tempted individuals over the centuries to manufacture theories to fit the name.

Domesday Book, compiled in 1086, makes no explicit reference to Oswestry. It does, however, mention a castle, L'oeuvre, built by Rainald, the sheriff of Shropshire, which is believed to be the newly-constructed Oswestry Castle. It also mentions a church. The sheriff, Rainald de Bailleul, held his lands as sub-tenant of Roger de Montgomeri, Earl of Shrewsbury. Until about 1085, both the lands and the sheriffdom had been held by Warin the Bald, who had died shortly before Domesday Book's compilation. Warin's son Hugh–Hugh FitzWarin–held the position of sheriff briefly at the close of the century.[6]

Domesday Book gives no hints as to the dedication of the church. However, the earliest surviving reference to the 'church of St Oswald', contained within one of the documents which comprise the

Shrewsbury Abbey counted Oswestry parish church amongst its possessions. It had the right to appoint its nominees as vicar of Oswestry. This view of the Abbey Church, dated 1811, was engraved by John Greig from a drawing by James Sargent Storer.

7

cartulary of Shrewsbury Abbey, dates back to the years immediately after Domesday Book's completion. The Rev. Eyton, in his multi-volume *Antiquities of Shropshire*, and the Rev. Thomas, in his *History of the Diocese of St Asaph*, both point to the grant made to Shrewsbury Abbey by Warin the Bald "of the church of St Oswald with the tithes of the same vill", as that earliest reference, giving it the date 1086.[7] Generally, this view has been adopted by subsequent writers, but recent research upon Shrewsbury Abbey's charters suggests that the charter in question, the so-called foundation charter of the Earl Roger, is spurious, concocted by a monk of the Abbey in the first half of the 12th century.[8] That being the case, the grant of St Oswald's to Shrewsbury Abbey was made ever so slightly later, jointly by Rainald de Bailleul and Hugh FitzWarin at some point between 1086 and 1098, probably whilst Shropshire was in the hands of the Earl Hugh, who had succeeded his father Roger de Montgomeri as Earl of Shrewsbury in 1094.[9]

It is interesting to note that the Normans dedicated their new church to St Oswald, who had been a Saxon King, even if he was by now a saint with an international reputation. Without wishing to enter the debate over the whereabouts of Maserfield–whether King Oswald really did fight King Penda of Mercia in what is now north Shropshire, or whether the battle took place at Winwick in Lancashire[10]–it is clear that there was something in the Oswestry area to prompt the Normans to adopt King Oswald for their parish church. What acted as that prompt may have been simply a well, a small chapel, or another church. Eyton suggests that the church might have transferred from Maesbury,[11] that a Saxon church serving the district from its pre-Conquest caput of Maesbury was transferred to the new caput of Oswestry, where a brand-new Norman church was built, and that the new church inherited its predecessor's Saxon dedication.

The adoption, at an early stage in Oswestry's history, of St Oswald's feast day of August 5th for the town's first annual fair, is another sign of a local cult. Isaac Watkin speculates that this fair was established in Saxon times,[12] although its existence is not documented until 1272, when an Inquisition into the affairs of John FitzAlan III listed the income of an annual fair of three days' duration.[13] Watkin's speculation might perhaps be well founded, but, if so, the Saxon fair must have moved to Oswestry, the new caput, in early Norman times.

Records maintained by Shrewsbury Abbey include information relating to the parish church and to the Abbey's property and estates in Oswestry. These provide a small amount of evidence on St Oswald's from the time of its foundation through to the dissolution of the monasteries. Similarly, other details are contained within Haughmond Abbey's records, largely the result of Haughmond's involvement in the foundation and administration of St John's hospital, set up by Bishop Reyner of St Asaph at the start of the 13th century and situated on the immediate outskirts of Oswestry.[14] Even so, contemporary documents, whether local or not, say very little about the staffing of the typical parish church prior to the 13th century. Often, small churches would have had only one priest; more sizeable parishes such as Oswestry would have had additional assistant clergymen, commonly known as chaplains. Oswestry's parish church, in its early years, is believed to have been a collegiate establishment, with its ecclesiastical functions carried out by a team of clerks rather than by a rector, vicar or single priest-in-charge. There have been suggestions that this situation reflected pre-Norman collegiate arrangements, either at Maesbury or Llanforda.[15] It is thought that St Oswald's clerks were regular canons or, more likely, secular canons. The Rev. Walcott,[16] writing in 1876, cited as evidence Mr John Davies of Middleton who, in 1635, had described how Bishop Reyner "in the reigne of Henry the second ... bestowed all the ... hay and corn of

Haughmond Abbey administered St John's hospital in Oswestry from the 13th to 16th century. The Abbey was founded by William FitzAlan I, Lord of Oswestry .
This view, of 1783, was engraved by Thomas Bonner.

Blank-monastery and the Chappels thereunto belonging where with were wonte to be maintayned twelve secular priests that for the moste parte hadd their lawfull wives upon the Monkes of Shrewsbury and by the Pope's authority expelled the said seculars." Mr Davies, in his turn, was citing the Bishop of Llandaff, Francis Godwin, whose *Catalogue of the Bishops of England* was first published in 1601. However, the clear evidence, as opposed to the speculation, is extremely sparse.

. It has already been noted that the parish church was presented to Shrewsbury Abbey towards the close of the 11th century. The 'foundation charter', now thought to be false, indicated that "the tithes of the same vill" had been handed over as part of the initial gift. Evidence from other, genuine, records of Shrewsbury Abbey is far less precise. It is clear that Shrewsbury Abbey, like most other religious houses, was constantly seeking to maximise the income from its estates; in this respect, the churches and chapels in the Abbey's possession were treated no differently to its other holdings of land and property. The aforementioned foundation charter can be seen as a retrospective attempt to provide written proof that the tithes had indeed been granted to the Abbey along with the church. Quite possibly, this freshly produced evidence was then exploited by the Abbey during the 1140s to gain from the Bishop of Chester confirmation that it possessed the tithes of a number of Shropshire churches including St Oswald's. In addition, the Bishop confirmed that parish clergy appointed to these churches had to pay an annual pension to the Abbey: in Oswestry's case, this was to be 30 shillings.[17] In fact, it was William FitzAlan II who presented the Abbey with two-thirds of the lord's demesne tithes, as a contribution to building work there; the remaining third was to support Oswestry's parish church and its clergy.[18] William FitzAlan's gift was subsequently confirmed by the Bishop of St Asaph,[19] evidence that the parish of Oswestry had passed from Chester to St Asaph at about this time. Oswestry was destined to remain an important part of the diocese of St Asaph until Welsh disestablishment brought about its transfer to Lichfield in 1920.

Shrewsbury Abbey also claimed possession of the advowson to St Oswald's: the right to appoint the priest, or priests, to the church. As with the question of tithes, the Abbey had claimed this right of nomination from the late 11th century; indeed, the Bishop of Chester's charters of confirmation, discussed above, speak clearly of Oswestry's clergy being appointed by the Abbey. It is perhaps significant that, during the 1140s and early 1150s , Shrewsbury Abbey would not have had the FitzAlans to gainsay their claims, as William FitzAlan I, who had taken the Empress Matilda's side against King Stephen, did not return from exile until 1154. On his return, by now an old man, William recognized the Abbey's possession of the advowson,[20] a state of affairs confirmed by his son William FitzAlan II.[21] However, the FitzAlans' relationship with Shrewsbury Abbey was not always so amicable, and, in the mid-13th century, John FitzAlan II, and his son John FitzAlan III, disputed vigorously the Abbey's rights to certain land holdings: the FitzAlans were alleged to have "ejected the abbot from his property, had levelled the abbot's houses, and appropriated the abbot's goods to the value of 60 merks."[22] They had also denied the Abbot his right to the advowson: in 1269, John FitzAlan III presented to the living his nominee Walter de Engemere, an appointment recognized by the Bishop of St Asaph. The Abbot of Shrewsbury fought hard to retain the Abbey's rights and privileges; he appealed first to Canterbury, then to Rome. Eventually, the case was settled 'out of court', with the Abbey's rights over St Oswald's restored, but only after the Abbot had compensated the Bishop of St Asaph with sizeable land holdings in St. Martins.

The Abbey's close interest in St Oswald's reflected national and international trends in ecclesiastical organisation. The religious orders increasingly were concerned to generate additional income: they were in debt; they needed to finance

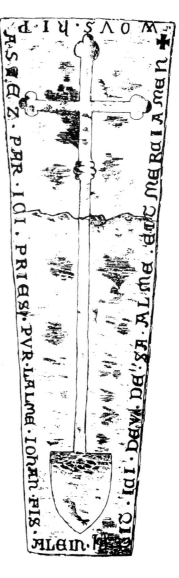

The monument to John FitzAlan III, Lord of Oswestry, discovered in the ruins of Haughmond Abbey in 1811. John FitzAlan appointed his nominee Walter de Engemere as vicar of Oswestry in 1269. A drawing by W. A. Leighton of Shrewsbury, dated 1825.

ambitious building projects, with stone replacing wood, with Gothic architecture replacing the Romanesque; popes and kings were demanding ever larger sums in taxation; and travellers were making ever greater use of monastic hospitality. From the early 13th century, bishops had to concern themselves more and more with monastic endeavours to 'appropriate' the income of churches under their patronage. Appropriation meant the sharp division of a church's income into two parts; one part was added to the patron's income (as rector), the other was allotted to the parish priest, known as the vicar. As resources attached to a living were often appreciably more than those needed to support a vicar, the patron (in Oswestry's case, the Abbey) stood to benefit from the surplus revenue. The fifteen years from about 1210 to 1225 saw a concerted move by Shrewsbury Abbey, which ended with the full appropriation of St Oswald's to the Abbey, quickly followed by the appointment of Oswestry parish church's first vicar, Philip FitzLeofth. This vigorous campaign is attested in great detail in Shrewsbury Abbey's own records, and provides further valuable evidence of the staffing of St Oswald's prior to the appointment of a vicar. Thus, when Bishop Reyner granted the Abbot, Hugh de Lacy, an annual pension of 20 marks from the income of St Oswald's, the Abbot agreed to present three suitable clerks, or chaplains, to carry out the duties of the church.[23] Shortly afterwards, when Reyner conceded to the Abbey the full appropriation of St Oswald's, and access to the parish church's third of the demesne tithes, the charter was witnessed by three local clerks, Odelou the chaplain, Stephen the cellarer, and Reginald "sacristan of the white minister."[24] Perhaps the latter was the same 'Reginald the clerk' who acted as witness to various of the second William FitzAlan's charters, including Oswestry's first civic charter, of 1190.

The rights and duties of the new vicar Philip FitzLeofth were set out by Bishop Reyner in a document dated December 29th 1223, and witnessed by John FitzAlan I.[25] Another document[26] of the same period specifies that the vicar was to have all the oblations, offerings, lesser tithes due to the church, together with three messuages in Oswestry, then in the possession of the vicar himself, "Hugo Belle" and "Johannes cute." Philip was to see that the church was served in a proper manner by two chaplains. All the greater tithes, land and rents were henceforth to pass direct to the Abbey. Barring the dispute fifty years on between the Abbey and the temporal lords FitzAlan, the monks of Shrewsbury had triumphed, and, until the demise of the religious orders in the late 1530s, the bulk of the income of St Oswald's, largely derived from land,

The inconspicuous lancet window in the church's west wall is probably the oldest feature surviving within the body of the church. It is believed to be of the 13th century.

property, produce and commerce in the Oswestry area, henceforth found its way to Shrewsbury, to the Abbey of St Peter and St Paul.

What, then, did the parish church look like in the 13th century, in the days of Bishop Reyner, Philip FitzLeofth, and the three Johns FitzAlan? What clues to the layout and appearance of the mediaeval church still survive? Unfortunately, there are very few, quite probably a consequence of Oswestry's Welsh border location, and its status as a frontier town, which caused it to be the scene of violent assault on many occasions, never more so than in the 13th century, when first King John attacked the town in 1216, then Llywelyn the Great put the town to the torch in 1233, and, finally, in the wars of Welsh independence against King Edward I, Oswestry was attacked twice more, notably on Palm Sunday 1282. It comes as no surprise that efforts were made from 1257 onwards to raise funds to build a defensive wall around the town, although it is somewhat surprising that the wall which was eventually constructed left both the church and St John's hospital outside. It has, however, been suggested that lack of funds forced a scaling down of the project, and, under the initial plans, the walls would have taken in the church.[27]

There is no proof that St Oswald's was ever attacked during these assaults–neither is there proof that the church escaped harm–but there is clear evidence of 13th century construction work upon the parish church, which sheds a certain amount of light on the church's former layout. That evidence is the so-called Norman tower, thought to be of early 13th century construction in its lower storeys,[28] and a stretch of church wall between the tower and the west door.

The Rev. Cranage, writing at the start of the present century, described the tower as "a deeply interesting building."[29] He wrote of "its peculiar position, almost inside the south aisle", stating that, "it is difficult to say how it stood in reference to the early mediaeval church.

13

As there is no connecting arch, it is possible that the tower was built as an addition to a Norman or Saxon building and it may have been quite separate from it." There is force to this argument, as the tower is buttressed all around, and the stonework at the base of the tower's eastern side (beside the south door), within the body of the present church, clearly looks like an external wall, particularly once the memorial tablets, which adorn its lower courses, are discounted: in the main, they were moved here from other parts of the church, notably the south transept, during Mr Street's restoration programme. The tower has something of a military feel to it: one can speculate that it was built by masons more used to building castles.

Taking the theory a stage further, one might suggest that, if the tower was built in the early 13th century, and its eastern flank was indeed an external wall at that time, then the side aisle between tower and south transept must have been a later addition. In the north aisle, the 17th century style windows, faithful Victorian copies of the originals, suggest a post-mediaeval widening of the church. However, the narrow lancet window at the west end, and the abnormal thickness of the wall at this point, indicate clearly that the west end of the church occupies the same line of ground today as it did in the 13th century. One can perhaps speculate that the 13th century St Oswald's followed a simple cruciform pattern, with nave, chancel, north and south transepts, and a tower added on at the church's south western corner. Externally the tower would have been white-washed, hence the name 'Blancminster': "the faire or white monasterie, soe termed of the collor wherewith the outside was lymed or plastered all over, whereby it app'red white a far of to the behoulders."[30] At the church's east end, there may by the 13th century have been side chapels, to the north and south of the main chancel, though it is more likely that these may have been added during the following 150 years.

What, though, of John Leland's cloister, which supposedly could be recalled by Oswestrians alive in the 1530s? Evidence of monastic buildings–cloister, lodging, or refectory–is non-existent. What information there is points towards a secular establishment rather than a monastery. Nevertheless, if there was indeed a college of twelve priests, with their wives and families, they would have required accommodation of some kind, and their property may well have been inherited by the vicar and assistant clergy appointed to St Oswald's from 1223; it has already been noted that one of the documents drawn up at the appointment of Philip FitzLeofth as vicar referred to three messuages:

these might have formed part of an ecclesiastical close, adjacent to the church. Evidence is very thin: other references are limited, and imprecise. For instance, Mr William Price, in his history of Oswestry, of 1815,[31] described "a spot of ground near the church, still called Erw Myneich, that is Monk's Acre; and, as the ancient name of the church was Blanc-minster, there can be little doubt that the monastery was adjoining to the church." In a tantalising aside, he added, "Some traces of the foundations are still discoverable, in digging graves in the churchyard."

To sum up, it is known that the parish church was granted by the Normans to Shrewsbury Abbey. Vicars were appointed, from 1223 onwards. Few traces remain of the mediaeval church, and there is much that can only be conjecture and speculation, from the Norman Conquest through to the Reformation. Unlike many other ancient churches, St Oswald's is unable to display a comprehensive list of incumbents from 1223 to date. In fact, prior to the dissolution of the monasteries, historians know the names of less than ten vicars of Oswestry: no such records survive at St Asaph, or amongst Shrewsbury Abbey's documents. We are limited instead to isolated references within public records, manorial surveys, and chance entries in the papers of Haughmond and Shrewsbury Abbeys.

It is only with the Reformation, the winding up of the religious orders, the chantries and the fraternities, carried out under both King Henry VIII and his son Edward VI, that new light can be shed upon developments at St Oswald's. The detailed survey of monastic income known as the Valor Ecclesiasticus, of 1536, recorded Shrewsbury Abbey's continued possession of the rectory of St Oswald's, noting that it was then worth £66 per annum. The vicarage was shown to be worth £23 per annum.[32]

With the dissolution, the rectory passed to the Crown, with whom it remained until 1611. However, evidence from 'an old survey' of Oswestry,[33] probably compiled during the reign of Edward VI, shows how the FitzAlans moved very quickly to re-establish their influence over St Oswald's; the survey noted unequivocally that "the Lordes and their ancestors had the parsonage of Oswestrey and certain tenements and Lands to the value of 10 pounds yearly called St Oswaldes Fieldes, in his or their owne handes and how it went to the said Abbey it is to be enquired of." Shortly afterwards, early in the reign of Queen Mary, the advowson formally was granted to Henry FitzAlan, Earl of Arundel.[34] Just as the new Queen had remained loyal to the Roman Catholic faith, so the FitzAlans retained a clear sympathy for the old order. Likewise,

Doctor William Morgan, successively Bishop of Llandaff and St Asaph, was vicar of Oswestry from 1599 to 1602. A portrait by Thomas Prytherch.

the vicar of Oswestry during much of this troubled period, Mr John Price, a FitzAlan appointment, aroused certain suspicions: in 1575, Government agents interrogated him, suspecting that he was in contact with Welsh Roman Catholics exiled to the continent, and that he had helped to conceal Hugh Owen, a Catholic priest, saving him from arrest.[35]

In 1585, Henry FitzAlan's grandson Philip Howard, who had inherited the FitzAlans' Oswestry estates, was arrested and imprisoned in the Tower of London, for his Roman Catholicism. In 1589, he was attainted on a charge of high treason, with his estates, titles and possessions forfeited to the Crown. As a result, for the next twenty years, the Queen's ministers held both the advowson and the rectory of St Oswald's, and it was the Crown which, in 1599, appointed William Morgan, Bishop of Llandaff and well-known as the translator of the complete Bible into Welsh, as vicar of Oswestry. Almost certainly he carried out his parochial duties through curates, rather than in person, but his local ties can be verified by an entry in St Oswald's parish register for January 1606, for the burial of Dr Morgan's widow Catherine.[36]

John Norden's survey of the Lordship of Oswestry, carried out in 1602 for Thomas Howard, Earl of Suffolk, recorded that, "Henry Earl of Arundel and his ancestors ... had the advowson and presentacion of the vicaredge of the sayde Towne of Oswestry."[37] Presumably this right passed to Suffolk, half-brother to the aforesaid Philip Howard, when he was granted the Lordship, manor and castle of Oswestry in 1603. In 1611, he acquired the rectory too, but thirteen years later, to assist him to pay off huge debts built up elsewhere, Suffolk sold all his rights and possessions in the Oswestry area to Dame Elizabeth Craven, widow of Sir William Craven of London. From the Craven family, these rights, including the rectory and advowson of St Oswald's, descended by marriage to the Earls of Powis.

Returning briefly to the Valor, it is interesting to note that it includes details relating to St Nicholas's chapel, situated within Oswestry Castle; Shrewsbury Abbey, presumably as part of its responsibilities as rector, had to find 100 shillings a year towards the cost of the chaplain, then a Richard Meredith, to celebrate masses in the chapel "for the soul of the Earl of Arundel."[38] The aforesaid 'old survey' shows the former chaplain being in receipt of an annual pension of £5.[39]

The Reformation had still further to go. After the dispersal of the main religious orders, and the seizure of their lands and property by the Crown, the reformers turned their attention to the smaller scale elements of the old order. The 1547 Chantries Act placed the lands and possessions of the countless chantry chapels, lay fraternities and religious guilds in the Crown's hands. These were chapels and side altars within parish churches, established and endowed by a local worthy, or by a group of individuals, perhaps fellow-tradesmen, and usually employing the services of one or more priests to pray on behalf of the benefactor. The winding up of the chantries provided evidence, in the Chantry Certificates, of a number of such chapels and altars within Oswestry parish church.[40] There was "the Service of Our Lady, founded off certain lands and tenements heretofore given to the ffindinge of two prestes to celebrate att the aulter off Our Lady wythin the parisshe church of Oswestre, intended to continue for ever"; this service had been founded by Thomas FitzAlan, Earl of Arundel, at the start of the 15th century. There was "the service of the Roode, founded off one prest to celebrate

The sumptuous tomb-chest of Thomas FitzAlan, Earl of Arundel and Lord of Oswestry, within the FitzAlan Chapel at Arundel. The Earl, who died in 1415, established a chantry chapel, dedicated to Saint Mary, within Oswestry parish church.

17

att aulter of the Holy Rode" within the church; also "the ffraternitye off Saynt Kateryne, ffounded off one prest to celebrate at the aulter of Saynt Kateryne"; and "the Service of Saynt Mychel, founded off one prest to celebrate at the aulter of S. Michell." The Churchwardens' Accounts, which survive for the years 1579 to 1613, also include references to another, "St James' chancel."Add to these the priests employed at St Oswald's chapel, beside the Well, at St John's hospital, and at St Edith's chapel, and it becomes clear that Oswestry, in mediaeval times, would have had a sizeable body of priests in its midst.

The last named, St Edith's, is something of a mystery. Leland locates it "north est toward Chester" and "clene without the suburbes." The 'old survey' of the lordship, compiled in the 1540s, refers simply to the chapel of "St Edyth bylt by the vicar of Oswestry and releeved by the inhabitants of the said Towne",[41] whilst Norden, in 1602, includes within his survey the paragraph, "The heirs of John Trevor have in their occupacion as conceyled a little peece of ground called the Chapel Peece lying at the point of theire land betweene twoe highe wayes whereof the one leadeth towardes Westchester thother to Whittington parke ... There was sometime a Chappell stoode upon this peece now decayed and as I thinke the heires have no title to it."[42] It may be significant that the 1838 tithe map of Oswestry shows a field, in the general area of today's Unicorn Estate, labelled "chapel field."

During the reign of Edward VI, the changes which when taken together comprised the English Reformation were executed with particular Protestant zeal. The period was one of great uncertainty, especially for a parish such as Oswestry, far from the centre of events, but nevertheless susceptible to their effect. For instance, the endowments of the various chantries were seized by the Crown, and sold on to ambitious men, often from far afield. The properties attached to the chantry of the Rood, or Holy Cross, within St Oswald's were sold in 1553 to Daniel and Alexander Pert of Tewkesbury, and to John and William Dodyngton of London;[43] and in 1549 and 1550, the lands and properties which had serviced the chantry of Our Lady were purchased from the Crown by John Peryent and Thomas Reve, and by William Wynlowe and Richard Felde of London.[44] Local tenants found themselves with new landlords, who were often men much more adept than their predecessors at maximising their income.

At the same time, inventories were ordered of church plate and other valuable possessions held by the churches, and the Crown employed commissioners in each county to seize such belongings from all churches, leaving each a single chalice and a sufficient number of surplices. In many parishes, the plate disappeared even before an inventory could be made, before the Crown had a chance to seize its prize. In St Oswald's case, the Oswestry Corporation Records for 1548 reveal the sum of £12 18s 8d being handed over by Thomas Lloyd and Richard Jones, bailiffs of the town, to the Corporation, to be placed within its oak chest for safe keeping, the sum having been raised from "plat by them sold in london." At the same time, "Richard blodwall gent, lyften'ant of osestrie" handed over "one gret Crosse of Selver and gylt" and "Richard ap Je'nn one other crose with a senser of selvr."[45] This plate may have belonged either to St Oswald's, or to one of its individual chantries. Interestingly, an entry in the Corporation Records for the

The Yale Monument, currently located in St Oswald's north aisle. Formerly, the monument may have stood in the Lady Chapel of the pre-Civil War church.

following year, 1549, appears to show that some of the money raised in this manner was used to repair the church, with twenty shillings "delyvred to Richard Baker and Jo'n Glovr two of the wardens of the parysh church of Oswestre to be payd unto langley of Salop in pt of paym't ... for certain leadd for the said church."[46] William Langley, a Shrewsbury tailor, had purchased the premises and site of Shrewsbury Abbey in July 1546, from a pair of property speculators who had themselves acquired the property from the Crown;[47] clearly Mr Langley was now seeking to realise his assets. It seems that Oswestry's churchwardens had bought a quantity of second-hand lead, taken from the roofs of buildings of the very Abbey which had previously counted St Oswald's as one of its own possessions. The wheel had turned full circle.

The Churchwardens' Accounts, which survive for a short period half a century on from the events of the Reformation, show clearly that St Oswald's side chapels retained their mediaeval dedication into the 17th century. The Accounts include references to the Lady chancel, St

Michael's chancel, and St James' chancel, as well as the high chancel, though they do not mention a chapel dedicated to St Catherine, suggesting that, in the mediaeval church, the service of St Catherine was performed at an altar within another chantry chapel, probably that dedicated to the Virgin Mary. However, there is no documentary evidence to pin-point the locations of these chapels. One can speculate that St Mary's chancel was situated immediately to the north of the High Altar, although the Rev. Thomas believed it to have "occupied the space between the tower and the (south) transept."[48] The inscription upon the Yale Monument indicates that this Lady Chapel, wherever it was located, was demolished during the Civil War. St Michael's chancel appears, from entries within the Churchwardens' Accounts, sometimes to have been known as the scholars' chancel;[49] possibly it would have occupied the area just inside the south door, nearest to the Grammar School buildings. In respect of St James' chancel, the Churchwardens' Accounts indicate that it had one or more windows, a roof which was identifiably its own, and that its location was sufficiently attractive for parishioners such as Richard Williams of Church Street to pay 3s 4d to reserve a kneeling place there.[50] Arguably Mr Williams' kneeling place would have been found in a chapel immediately to the south of the High Altar: the location of today's Lady Chapel. Certainly, a reference in the Accounts to a "mydle chaunsell"[51] confirms that the pre-Civil War church had side chapels on both sides of the high chancel. Finally, the service of the Rood would have been performed at an altar on the western side–the nave side–of the rood screen: a screen commonly built across the church to separate the congregation from the 'mystery' of the altar, and generally dominated by a carved wooden crucifix, which would have been removed in accordance with an Act of Parliament of 1548. Access through the screen to the chancel was achieved via a door. The Accounts include various payments for repairs to the rood loft,[52] and to purchase a lock and key for the rood loft door.[53] Also, in 1603, the Weavers' Company of Oswestry is recorded as paying the sum of 6s 8d for a kneeling place "hard by the Dore that goeth to the Rood Loft provided that the Dore is to be used at all Tymes."[54]

Therefore, in the years immediately preceding the Civil War, Oswestry had its parish church situated outside the town walls, in a strategic position alongside the main road to Welshpool. The church was large, with several side chapels, and with an impressive steeple. The Churchwardens' Accounts indicate that the church had a peal of bells, an organ, and a newly installed church clock. It had glazed windows: there is no evidence to show whether these incorporated stained glass. Inside, the church walls were white-washed. The church floor was paved largely with gravestones, so much so that the Accounts for 1608 included a memorandum "that it is agreed by and between the parishioners of Oswestry that none shalbe buried in the church of Oswestry without the consent of the vickar and church wardens of the sd church unless they bee men or women of good sort quality and estate."[55] Generally, it was a well maintained church, possibly in consequence of the prosperity and well-being within Oswestry, engendered by the weekly wool and cloth market.

Oswestry was a Royalist town at the start of the Civil War. However, the inadequacies of the town's defences–the castle, town walls, and surrounding ditch–had been well recognized long before hostilities broke out: John Norden had described their poor state of repair in great detail in his report to the Earl of Suffolk in 1602. Certainly, the Royalist governor of the town, Edward Lloyd of Llanforda, would have expended both time and money in strengthening the barricades prior to conflict breaking out. Nevertheless, when hostilities began, the 'battle of Oswestry', of June 22nd and 23rd 1644, was over quickly and resulted in defeat for the Crown, victory for the forces of Parliament. The demolition of Oswestry Castle, and of the town walls, followed after. And the parish church? According to Pevsner, it "suffered badly in the Civil War."

Thomas Pennant, writing in the late 18th century, described how "the governor had fortified (the town) very strongly; and lest the enemy should annoy it from the steeple, pulled it down to the body of church, part of which he also demolished."[56] The inscription upon the Yale Monument tells of Hugh and Dorothy Yale, "interred within ye chancel of this church commonly called St Mary's before its demolition in the late wars", whilst a Parliamentary Inquisition of 1655 described a church "now at present wholie demolished by Order of the Comittee of the

Major Gen: Mitton

Colonel Thomas Mytton of Halston. From John Vicars' England's Worthies.

21

Sir Thomas Myddelton of Chirk (1586-1666). A portrait in the manner of Robert Walker.

Countie of Salop for pr'servation of the garrison then in the Parliam'ts possession. The Vicarage house beinge then allso demolished."[57] Another description, by Richard Gough of Myddle, who had close relatives living in Oswestry at the time of the Civil War, tells how "the Governor of this Towne when it was a Garrison for the King pulled downe many houses that were without the Wall lest they might shelter an enemy. The Church also beeing without the Wall was pulled downe, and the toppe of the Steeple unto that loft where the bell-frame stood. The bells were brought into the Towne and the Organs were imbezzled."[58]

It seems clear, therefore, that St Oswald's steeple was pulled down well before battle commenced, and by forces of the King rather than any Parliamentary army. For facts upon the conflict, and its impact upon the church, we are fortunate that the chief protagonists from the Parliamentary side recorded their thoughts upon the hostilities in journals or in letters, details of which have survived. Thus, when the Earl of Denbigh approached Oswestry on Saturday June 22nd with his Parliamentary troops, he found the church "well manned"; "Our Foot made an onslaut on the church being but 200, and in an half hours sore fight entred the church, the enemie fled into the steeple, thence they fetcht them down with a powder; there we took 27 prisoners", he noted.[59] The evidence of his colleague, Colonel Thomas Mytton of Halston, backs this up; "wee were forced first to take the church, wherein there was 25", he wrote.[60] Mytton then "planted his cannon neare that part of the steeple which was left."[61] The castle fell the following morning, after which, "it being the Lord's day", the victors were called away "to go to Church to praise God, which was done, and our dead buried."[62]

Less than a fortnight later, the Royalists were back, and in far larger numbers–1,500 horse, 3,500 foot–under a Colonel Marrow, who laid siege to Oswestry, in an attempt to recapture it. The Royalist forces recaptured the church, but failed to retake the town: Sir Thomas Myddelton of Chirk described how "the enemy before the relief came had taken the church being the strongest hold about the town. Upon the approach of the relief they suddenly deserted it, and sent their two battering peeces unto Shrewsbury."[63]

Evidence on the ground does not quite coincide with the recorded evidence of Denbigh, Mytton and Myddelton. Their concentration upon damage to the church tower and steeple has encouraged subsequent generations to adopt views along the lines of Nikolaus Pevsner, that only the lower part of the present tower is mediaeval, with the rest built after the Civil War. Whilst the tower's south door, dated 1692, the uppermost storey and balustrade support this point of view, it is contradicted by the evidence inside the church tower. Just as the tower's ground and first floor exterior walls, particularly on its southern flank, reveal several different phases of construction, so does the stonework inside the tower, on the present first floor, second floor, and, most significantly, on the floor above. Here, in the room which houses the clock mechanism, just below the bell frame, the springers or squinches which formerly supported the base of the steeple survive in three of the four corners of the tower. The fact that the south eastern springer has not survived may indicate that a more thorough job was made of pulling down the steeple in that corner. Gough states specifically that the Royalist garrison pulled down the steeple "unto that loft where the bell-frame stood", and it seems that he was an accurate witness in this respect. It should also be noted that the springers survive on either side of the tower's north window, just above it, adding weight to the argument that the window is older than many believe. The local architect W. H. Spaull

A mediaeval springer, in the church tower's north eastern angle. Masonry of this kind, at each of the tower's four corners, would have supported a spire or steeple prior to its dismantling in the Civil War.

23

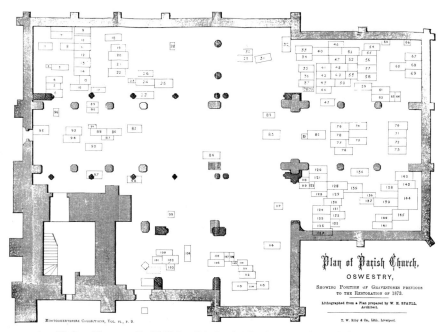

Plan of Parish Church,
OSWESTRY,
SHOWING POSITION OF GRAVESTONES PREVIOUS
TO THE RESTORATION OF 1873.

Lithographed from a Plan prepared by W. H. SPAULL,
Architect.

MONTGOMERYSHIRE COLLECTIONS, VOL. VI., P. 9.

T. W. Riby & Co., Lith. Liverpool.

A plan of St Oswald's prepared by W. H. Spaull during the Victorian restoration work of 1872-1874. The dark shading in nave and transept represents Mr Street's new pillars and arches which generally replaced their mediaeval and 17th century predecessors at this time. The numbered squares indicate the position of gravestones which made up a large part of the church floor prior to the installation of the present Victorian tiles.

thought this window to be of the 13th century.[64]

The survival of the squinches proves that the tower survived the Civil War, to a significant height at least. Its interior still exhibits clear signs of its mediaeval origins; indeed, it is only in the tower that one can still see the different stages of building and rebuilding, evident in the tower's external south wall, in the relationship of the three round-headed windows on the second floor to adjacent stonework, in the shutting-off of the lower courses of the spiral staircase, and in the blocking-up of two round arched windows (possibly a window and an external doorway) on the tower's western flank. This last mentioned work appears to have been forced upon the church by the need to erect a central buttress on that side of the tower, quite possibly in the immediate post-Civil War period. The tower as a whole would clearly repay a detailed architectural and archaeological survey.

That so much survives undoubtedly owes much to the Victorians, who chose to exclude the tower from their extensive restoration projects. The body of the church fared somewhat differently, being transformed by the work of G. E. Street. Although there is written evidence to suggest that Street swept from view various mediaeval features of the church–particularly three arches to the western end of the nave, and perhaps the former south door–it is clear that the church had already been substantially rebuilt in the late 17th century, after the Civil War. In 1657, a Brief was issued authorising a collection "towards the rebuilding of the church of Oswestree which in the late wars was demolisht and layd even with the ground, the inhabitants being without a meeting place for the publique worship of God."[65] A second Brief was issued in 1675,[66] seeking a further £1,500, and a third Brief in 1691, for another £2,800.[67] This third Brief refers to damage caused by fire within the church; interestingly, a Terrier of St Oswald's lands, properties and tithes, dated 1685 and part of St Asaph's diocesan records, refers to "a vicarage house which was burnt and demolished to the ground in the late wars; vidt. in the year of our lord 1644 or thereabouts, when the church was pulled down and many buildings burnt, upon the account of a siege laid to the same town, being then a garrison."[68]

Clearly the church as a whole suffered great damage during the Civil War. The Shropshire Quarter Sessions in 1655 were advised that, "the charge of the rebuilding of the parish church of Oswestry will amount to £7,000 at the least",[69] an immense sum, which, from the evidence of the Briefs, was only

The lower part of the church tower, from the south. At least three distinct periods of construction, or of restoration, are clearly visible.

raised in stages. No doubt the first stage, carried out in the late 1650s and early 1660s, included the most urgent work, to make the church structurally sound; in addition, it included the installation of a new font, presented by Colonel Lloyd of Llanforda, and dated 1662. The Churchwardens' Accounts for August 30th 1677 show that work to the tower and steeple had continued into the late 1670s;[70] other work from this time included a new altar of 1672 (transferred to St David's, Welsh Walls, in the 19th century), and the restoration of the Yale Monument. It is quite possible that the oft-quoted date 1616, supposedly the date that the monument was first set up, is in reality 1676, the date of its restoration.[71] The third Brief of 1691 is represented by the tower's external door of 1692 and, it is generally thought, by the upper storey and balustrade to the tower. Cranage thought the tower's north window to be Jacobean Gothic and of this general period of restoration,[72] as were the predecessors of the present north aisle windows, and the whole of the east end of the church. The scale of the work involved in this restoration, coupled with the less prosperous state of the local economy after the Civil War, caused much of the work to be of a very basic standard, described by Victorian commentators as "rudely constructed and ill

'Oswestry Church from the South West' by David Parkes (1763-1833), an illustration which appeared in the Gentleman's Magazine *of 1810. One of the earliest surviving views of St Oswald's, it is unfortunately far from accurate.*

proportioned masses of wall masonry",[73] with the "roof and arches of the meanest character possible."[74] Most of this work was, in any case,completely swept away during the Victorian rebuilding of St Oswald's.

The font, in the north aisle, presented to the church by Edward Lloyd (1609-1663) in 1662. It bears the double-headed eagle crest of the Lloyds of Llanforda.

No one would argue that Oswestry parish church, the building bequeathed to current generations by the Victorian restorers, is an architectural gem, to be placed alongside St Laurence's in Ludlow, St Bartholomew's of Tong, St Mary's of Shrewsbury, or, say, St Melangell's chapel at the head of the Tanat valley. Neither would one argue that St Oswald's, in its pre-Victorian guise, would have been so placed. Purely in terms of architectural interest, the present St Oswald's is not in the same league, and we know too little of the church's appearance before the ravages of the Civil War, and the changes of the Reformation, to be able to speculate whether it ever was the architectural equal of those churches. Nevertheless, it is an important church, and, in terms of its history, even in the incomplete form that we know it, St Oswald's would bear comparison with the best.

NOTES

1. N. Pevsner, *The Buildings of England, Shropshire* (London, 1958), p222-223.
2. L. T. Smith (ed.), *The Itinerary of John Leland in or about the years 1535-1543*, III (London, 1907), p73-76.
3. T. Pennant, *Tour in Wales*, I (London, 1784), p260-261. Pennant refers to Bishop Thomas Tanner's *Notitia Monastica* of 1695. Tanner was Bishop of St. Asaph.
4. J. A. Roberts, 'Oswestry ecclesiastical history: the old church', *Transactions of the Shropshire Archaeological Society*, III (1880), p175-212. See in particular p177; it should be stressed that the suggestion was not that of Mr Roberts.
5. The Rev. Robert Williams, *Enwogion Cymru: a biographical dictionary of eminent Welshmen* (Llandovery, 1852), p337.
6. F. & C. Thorn, *Domesday Book: Shropshire* (Chichester, 1986).
7. The Rev. R. W. Eyton, *Antiquities of Shropshire*, X (London, 1854-60), p319; the Rev. D. R. Thomas, *History of the Diocese of St. Asaph* (London, 1874), p644.
8. U. Rees, *Cartulary of Shrewsbury Abbey*, I (Aberystwyth, 1975), p5-7.
9. Ibid., p31-39.
10. See J. A. Roberts, 'Where did King Oswald die?', *T.S.A.S.*, II (1879), p97-140.
11. Eyton, X, p335.
12. I. Watkin, *Oswestry, with an account of its old houses, shops etc.* (Oswestry, 1920), p101.
13. P.R.O. C.132/42/5.
14. See in particular U. Rees, *Cartulary of Haughmond Abbey* (Cardiff, 1985).
15. Eyton, X, p335; Thomas, p650.
16. *T.S.A.S.*, III (1880), p178-179. Walcott refers to J. Davies, *Observations on the antient and moderne names of the Towne and Borrough of Oswestrie* (1635), Harleian MS 1981, printed in part in J. Y. W. Lloyd, *History of the princes, lords marcher and ancient nobility of Powys Fadog*, VI (London, 1881-87).
17. Rees, *Cartulary of Shrewsbury Abbey*, II (Aberystwyth, 1975), p297-299.
18. Ibid., p280-281; Eyton, X, p335. This grant has been dated only to the broad period 1186-1210.
19. Rees, p327-328. A further document suggests that St Oswald's may also have been linked to the Diocese of Coventry & Lichfield

during the 12th century: see Rees, p329.

20. Ibid., p285.
21. Ibid., p280-281.
22. Thomas, p647. The dispute is described by Eyton, X, p339-341, and documented by Rees, p62, p324-327, p334.
23. Rees, p332.
24. Ibid., p282.
25. Ibid., p322-323.
26. Ibid., p328.
27. D. Pratt, *Oswestry town wall* (Oswestry, 1981), p4-5.
28. The Rev. D. H. S. Cranage, *An Architectural account of the churches of Shropshire* (Wellington, 1908), p810.
29. Ibid., p814.
30. Davies, *Observations etc.* (1635).
31. W. Price, *History of Oswestry from the earliest period* (Oswestry, 1815), p11.
32. Record Commission (ed.), *Valor Ecclesiasticus,* IV (London, 1821), p448-449. See also Eyton, X, p342-343; Thomas, p648.
33. W. Slack (ed.), *Lordship of Oswestry* (Shrewsbury, 1951), p12.
34. *Calendar of Patent Rolls, 1553-54* (London, 1937), p184.
35. *Calendar of State Papers, Domestic,1547-80* (London, 1856), p504-505; *Bye Gones,* 18th March 1903, p54-55.
36. W. Day (ed.), *The Churchwardens' Accounts for 1579-1613* (Oswestry, 1970), p125, p129; Shropshire Parish Register Society, *Oswestry Registers,* I (Shrewsbury, 1909), p264. In 1601, Doctor Morgan was appointed Bishop of St Asaph; he resigned as Vicar of St Oswald's in 1602.
37. Slack, p48.
38. *Valor Ecclesiasticus,* IV (London, 1821), p449. The actual reference is to a 'free chapel within the church of Oswestry', though clearly the free chapel of St Nicholas within Oswestry Castle is intended. See Eyton, X, p345.
39. Slack, p12.
40. *T.S.A.S.,* III (1880), p179; see also A. H. Thompson, 'Certificates of the Shropshire Chantries under the Acts of Henry VIII and Edward VI', *T.S.A.S.,* 3rd Series, X (1910), p322-323, p353-355.
41. Slack, p12.
42. Ibid., p53.
43. *C.P.R., 1550-53* (1926), p313; Ibid., *1553* (1927), p148.
44. Ibid., *1549-51* (1925), p14-15, p284-285.

45. *Bye Gones*, 28th February 1877, p190.

46. Ibid.

47. H. Owen and J. B. Blakeway, *History of Shrewsbury*, II (Shrewsbury, 1825), p135-136.

48. Thomas, p650.

49. Day, p173, et passim.

50. Ibid., p 24, p83, p108.

51. Ibid., p204.

52. Ibid., p71, p103, et passim.

53. Ibid., p164.

54. Ibid., p103.

55. Ibid., p154-155. See also S. Leighton, 'A list of the monumental inscriptions which were in the Church of St Oswald in the year 1872', *Montgomeryshire Collections*, VII (1874), p1-36; this includes the plan by W. H. Spaull, which is featured on p 24 of the present publication.

56. Pennant, p270.

57. *T.S.A.S.*, XLVII (1933-34), p22-23.

58. R. Gough, *The History of Myddle*, written between 1700 and 1702, and first published in 1834. See p271 of the Penguin edition (1981). William Gough of Sweeney, who died in 1668, and is buried in St Oswald's, was Richard Gough's great uncle.

59. Cited in *Salopian Shreds and Patches*, 16th June 1875.

60. Ibid., 9th June 1875.

61. Gough, p271.

62. The Earl of Denbigh, cited in *S.S.P.*, 16th June 1875.

63. *S.S.P.*, 5th May 1875.

64. Watkin, p64, citing *Bye Gones*, 30th August 1893, p162; also 21st July 1897, p161.

65. Rev. D. R. Thomas, *History of the Diocese of St Asaph* (expanded edition), III (Oswestry, 1913), p53; Watkin, p67; see also *Bye Gones*, 3rd July 1895, p124; 2nd August 1905, p100.

66. *T.S.A.S.*, III (1880), p183; Thomas (1874 edition), p652; Watkin, p67-68.

67. Cranage, p816; *Bye Gones*, 24th August 1881, p287.

68. Price, p57.

69. Kenyon, R. Lloyd (ed.), *Abstracts of the Orders of the Shropshire Quarter Sessions, 1638-1708* (Shrewsbury, undated), p23.

70. Price, p103.

71. Hugh Yale was buried on January 9th 1606; his wife Dorothy is

known to have survived at least to 1609. Conceivably, Dorothy Yale died during 1611, a year in which the Vicar failed to maintain the parish register. See *Oswestry Registers,* I (Shrewsbury, 1909), p264; Day, p129, p139, p164.

72. Cranage, p815.
73. Thomas, p651.
74. *Bye Gones*, 27th August 1879, p276.

Saint Oswald's Well, reputedly the place where the martyr's arm fell to earth, having been dropped by a scavenging eagle, after the battle of Maserfield on August 5th 642.